ALEXANDER GLAZUNOV
CONCERTO FOR SAXOPHONE AND ORCHESTRA IN E-FLAT MAJOR, OP. 109

ERLAND VON KOCH
CONCERTO FOR SAXOPHONE AND ORCHESTRA IN E-FLAT MAJOR

Lawrence Gwozdz, *Saxophone*
The Plovdiv Philharmonic Orchestra
Nayden Todorov, *Conductor*

To access audio visit:
www.halleonard.com/mylibrary
Enter Code
6935-4197-0592-2284

ISBN 978-1-59615-605-0

EXCLUSIVELY DISTRIBUTED BY

HAL•LEONARD®
7777 W. BLUEMOUND RD. P.O. BOX 13819 MILWAUKEE, WI 53213

Visit Hal Leonard Online at
www.halleonard.com

ALEXANDER GLAZUNOV
SAXOPHONE CONCERTO IN E-FLAT MAJOR, OP. 109

Alexander Glazunov (1865–1936) was one of Russia's most respected Late Romantic composers, and one who bridged the gap between nineteenth-century Romantic style and twentieth-century "modernity." A pupil of Rimsky-Korsakov, he went on to teach Prokofiev and Shostakovich and became world-famous for his elegant compositions. His music is always filled with daring and unusual orchestrations and forms. After leaving Russia in 1928, he settled in Paris. It was during a concert tour in late 1929 that Glazunov heard Gershwin play his *Rhapsody in Blue* with the New York Philharmonic. He became fascinated by American jazz; this led to his enchantment with the saxophone's unique tonal qualities. The result was his now-famous saxophone concerto of 1933. Full of rich melodies and a beautiful orchestral fabric, this single-movement work remains one of the high points in saxophone literature, giving the soloist a magnificent opportunity to express himself against the rich backdrop of Glazunov's unique orchestrations.

ERLAND VON KOCH
SAXOPHONE CONCERTO IN E-FLAT MAJOR

A quarter-century after the premiere of Glazunov's saxophone concerto, in 1958, Swedish composer Erland von Koch (1910–2009) created another milestone in the genre—a three-movement piece for saxophone and orchestra exploiting the many tonal explorations made since that Russian composer's previous work. Its rich and unusual character, echoing the mid-twentieth-century fascination with dissonances, uses the solo instrument in extremely adventurous ways, including slap-tonguing, flutter tones, and broad use of the instrument's upper register. Von Koch stretches the bounds in creating a searing and steamy work which keeps the soloist in stark relief against the string orchestra. The influence of such composers as Bartok and Kodály is evident in the overall fabric of the piece. It is exciting, affecting music, using folk rhythms and melodies in a complex and arresting virtuoso piece for the saxophone.

CONTENTS

Alexander Glazunov: Concerto for Saxophone   6
and Orchestra in E-flat Major

Erland von Koch: Concerto for Saxophone and Orchestra in E-flat Major

     I. Allegro moderato   13

     II. Andante sostenuto   18

     III. Allegro vivace   20

A COMMENT ON THE PERFORMANCES

THE LISTENER will likely hear some deviations from the text in the soloist's interpretation of the concerti. This is the result of factual information gleaned from his several experiences with the dedicatee of both works, Sigurd Rascher.

In reference to the Glazunov, one will hear several differences in the solo apart from the cadenza. This is a reflection of what Glazunov originally composed. In the cadenza the soloist made a decision to extend a portion here and there for mere intensification, and this is to be considered optional.

In both concerti you will also notice that Lawrence Gwozdz is not a rationalist or single-minded literalist, but always opts for the most expressive way of playing any particular passage within the larger contours of the phrase at hand. Once upon a time this was called a "Romantic" style of playing, and has been the hallmark of many great instrumentalists of the past century. After the anti-romantic antics of a whole post-war generation (though many of them were great musicians), it is a pleasure to see a new generation open to the expressive possibilities that lie beyond the notes.

If you desire further information on each of these works, please consult the excellent periodical *The Saxophone Symposium* for the following articles:

Alexander Glazunov – Concerto pour Saxophone Alto avec l'orchestre de cordes (Sigurd Rascher, Spring 1988)

Dossier Glazunov (Jacques Charles, Summer 1988)

Erland von Koch and his Saxophone Concerto – Parts 1, 2, and 3 (Brian Ayscue, Spring, Summer, Fall 1983)

Glazunov's Saxophone Concerto

"Glazunov? Wasn't he some Russian poet?" is hardly an unlikely utterance even from more sophisticated music lovers these days. Such are, unfortunately, the vicissitudes of history, often a cruel mistress to those artists who endeavored to serve her well, indeed, did serve her well. Alexander Glazunov (1865-1936) was a man like this, immensely gifted, prophesied over, and playing the role of prophet at a time when many giants walked the earth. One of these patriarchal gladiators was the great Franz Liszt, who performed the anointing on Glazunov after hearing the young man's first symphony. Now, it is true that Liszt made many such pronouncements over the span of his long career, and often such a blessing was the kiss of death—few came to fruition. But he was on to something here, and perhaps the biblical axiom of a prophet never being accepted in his native land was never truer than in the case of Alexander Glazunov.

The composer has now been unfairly assigned to the endless category of Russian second-tier artists. How often are composers like Medtner, Arensky, or Taneyev played or listened to in our international concert halls? Even among the musically literate, the names are seldom mentioned aside from a few identifying works. During his life, Glazunov was heralded as a composer of great promise, but one problem dogged him then and continues to do so now—he is simply not as "Russian" as his illustrious predecessors. "The Mighty Five," the self-proclaimed inheritors of all things genuinely Slavic, did a most persuasive job in defining Russian music of the nineteenth century. Tchaikovsky arrived and bucked the trend to a degree, freely making use of the European musical inheritance while simultaneously writing a music that was more genuinely Russian than the "Five." Glazunov, perhaps the most cosmopolitan of all (save Glinka, perhaps), freely embraced the caresses of western musical history, openly adoring composers like Beethoven, and writing works that owed their structural elements more to the teachings of the Germans instead of someone like Rimsky-Korsakov.

This cosmopolitan worldview was hardly surprising considering his privileged upbringing. Glazunov, as a child blessed with a noble bloodline, was exposed early on to all of the benefits and intellectual wealth that Europe had to offer. By the age of seventeen he had already composed his first symphony and string quartet. By twenty-four he was a professor at the famous St. Petersburg Conservatory. Free of any financial fetters, his early years were a gift to the world of music—an amazingly fecund period that produced symphonies, ballets, quartets, concerti, and a host of smaller works.

At one point a strong musical reactionary, his devotion to the styles and manners of the nineteenth century seeped into his musical perspective, allowing him to form a real resistance to the persuasive trends of the day. But every significant moment in musical history has seen these same reactions, pro and con, with both sides of the debate always inundated with innovative, highly skilled composers. That Glazunov was a traditionalist there can be no doubt. But no more so than Brahms, another reactionary embracing conservatism (or at least a model of it). And it is equally certain that Glazunov's view of "Russian-ness" was one that incorporated a wide variety of internationalist flavors, maybe even more than the arch-heretic Stravinsky. His last years, spent in a Paris that he had known and loved, but one that had changed from a cross-century "comfortableness" to a musical environs dominated by the aforementioned Stravinsky, were not easy ones. Glazunov was devastated, feeling more respected than admired. And perhaps it was—and still is—true. Glazunov is not in the same league as Stravinsky (though he can hold his own among the "Mighty Five"), but few are; yet that doesn't mean that they should be written off altogether. How many classical-period composers were in the same league as Mozart? None, I would venture. Yet Glazunov did leave a large, largely untapped body of beautiful work that the world is surely poorer for if it continues to ignore it.

The Saxophone Concerto is one of Glazunov's last—and best—works, an incredibly concentrated score full of surprising twists and turns. The cover page says that the work is by "A. Glazunov et A. Petiot", but it has been long established that Andre Petiot had nothing to do with the genesis of this work, though some people remain under the delusion that he in fact composed the entire final allegro. The great Sigurd Rascher, the driving force behind the germination of the piece—and also its dedicatee—explains it thus: though the work is in one movement, it possesses three independent parts, following the traditional concerto model. But even this only hints at the riches found in this music. It is in fact a "metamorphosis" (again, Rascher's words) with the first movement neatly transformed almost into the last movement.

The broad, brooding, majestic theme of the introduction gives way to a variant in the saxophone's exposition that is modified even further in the second statement of this initial "theme." Glazunov tricks us into thinking that we are hearing a genuine sonata-form structure, when in reality we are presented with an exposition, and two two-part melodic statements that have the second half of each serving as a modified development of the first half. There is no real development as such in this section, making the term "concerto" somewhat of an affectation. It is much more sophisticated than a normal concerto.

The second section imitates the first with an introduction that is not only a variant of the introduction of the first section, but also a transition to the first theme of the "slow" section, in C-flat. This section also has two main thematic statements, but the second half of each in this case is more flowing and rhapsodic in style, though Glazunov will develop these motives later on in a very subtle manner. At the end of this section there is an extended cadenza. Glazunov again tips his hat to the concerto form while using it in a different manner for his own purposes. At the end of the cadenza, a fourteen-measure transition appears that steals its theme from the bass accompaniment of the second half of the second theme in section I! The man literally draws his ideas from the smallest of musical materials.

Section III, the infamous fughetta—because for many years it was imagined that Glazunov left off work here—explodes its initial statement so that the composer has us thinking we are in for some kind of enormous fugal episode. But his real motive is to familiarize us with the insistent triplet-loaded twelve-eight meter that he will ingeniously use to pit twos against threes in a very Brahmsian topsy-turvy rhythmical bacchanal. Glazunov again imitates the first movement's A-a B-b structure, each theme being a variant on its corresponding theme in the first section, moving into an extended coda that recapitulates many of the motives in a shifting cornucopia of melodic invention. By any measure, this work is a fluid, dynamically integrated list of ideas that constitute a unified whole, and proves that Glazunov, for all of his staid traditionalism, still had a very creative way of looking at things, even near the end of his life.

—Steven Ritter

MMO 4132

to Mr. Sigurd M. Rascher

CONCERTO
FOR
SAXOPHONE
AND
STRING
ORCHESTRA
ALEXANDER
GLAZUNOV
OP. 109

8

10

ERLAND VON KOCH'S SAXOPHONE CONCERTO

IT WILL FOREVER BE A MUSICOLOGICAL MYSTERY why some children inherit talent from their parents, while others have none, and still others seem to have it bestowed upon them like a pure gift from God. There is no doubt that God had a hand in the transmission, but Erland von Koch (1910-) seems to have been born with a double portion of talent encouraged by his famous father Sigurd, who was also his first teacher. His studies later continued at the Stockholm Conservatory of Music before embarking on a continental trip that landed him in France and Germany. Rare indeed is the talent that can measure up to the demands of Höffer (composition), Krause (conducting), and Arrau (piano). No mean student, this young von Koch kid! On returning to Sweden, he tried his way, with success, as a conductor, and took up a position at the Wohlfahrt Music School. Aside from a stint as a sound technician with the Swedish Radio in 1943—imagine the interests of this young prodigy, to be on the cutting edge of technology so early—he taught and eventually became professor at the Royal College of Music in Stockholm.

Von Koch paid particular attention to the music of Grieg, Sibelius, Bartok, and Kodaly, and from this we can glean the influences that would, one way or the other, influence his compositional method. His intense interest in Dalecarlian folk music, coupled with an uncanny ability to incorporate either raw folk melodies or folk-like melodies into his music made him a very popular composer abroad. Over the years his tonality broadened while he perfected his rhythmic and contrapuntal skills, especially in his use of variation technique. Among his noted works are the orchestral Oxberg Trilogy, Scandinavian Dances, and Swedish Polka. His vast output includes symphonies, ballets, operas, concerti, and a host of choral and chamber works. And, of course, the Saxophone Concerto.

Once again we must thank the indefatigable Sigurd Rascher, who was determined, at a concert in Sweden in 1958, to look up von Koch and discuss music with him. As has happened so often, after hearing Rascher play, von Koch decided to write a concerto for him. Mr. Rascher has played it all over the world ever since. A more suitable discmate to the Glazunov could hardly be found; indeed, von Koch's approach to the concerto, apart from obvious nationalistic and period influences, is remarkably similar to the older master's. One wonders how much time he may have spent delighting in the intricacies of the Glazunov. But where the latter enjoyed creating melodies and motives out of any and all musical constructs, feeding one another like fish in a food chain, von Koch is much more linear in his approach. There is a curious black-and-white quality to this work, not unlike much of Bartok. When the saxophone plays, the orchestra, for the most part, falls into a supporting role, emerging again only when the soloist is done. Only occasionally do they both meet, and these instances are very powerful musically. Glazunov, on the other hand, is continuously melding soloist and orchestra, so much so that you get the feeling that his concerto could have been revised in several ways, so flexible is the material.

This is not the case with von Koch. Nothing is wasted, everything is significant and unchangeable, and a rigorous constructionism formed by a marvelous economy of means is present everywhere. Movement one has been described in many ways since the appearance of this work in 1959. Fantasia is the word most often used, but I believe that the composer—like Glazunov—is teasing us with a modified sonata form. After an energetic two-measure introduction that more than sets the mood for the entire movement, the saxophone enters with its exposition that is a large, long,

breathless eight measure melodic line only slightly—but insistently—punctuated by orchestral interjections. The line is then repeated by the orchestra—including the two-bar intro—with the saxophone "ad-libing" over the top in a very neo-baroque manner. The second theme follows in the same manner, imitating the structural pattern exactly. At this point, the tease begins, when instead of a bona fide development, we get yet another principal theme (marked cantabile), followed by yet another theme—the count is now four!—before an honest development of the third theme begins. The saxophone continues its filigree part until we are presented with what appears to be a recapitulation, but—fooled again!—this time von Koch has the melody inverted, though you hardly notice because of the suppleness of the writing. The development continues until the saxophone caps a wonderful ten-measure crescendo that puts us in the recap proper. This is extraordinary writing, with all four initial themes recapitulated in order before a tremendously exerting cadenza.

Here we must pause to ponder some of von Koch's arsenal of musical materials. Despite affinities for Bartok and Kodály, and a phenomenal predilection for folk music, he is in the end a nationalist in the best sense of the word. Sweden, like many countries at that time, was waging a compositional war—always a tension between native nationalism and the riches to be absorbed through a more cosmopolitan outlook. Von Koch's heart belonged to his homeland, and like the composers mentioned above, this was to be the source of his inspiration. Modalities abound, especially the Dorian and Lydian. A multitude of open chords involving fourths and fifths are to be found, infusing a sort of stark, primitive, chant-like quality into the music. In the concerto he exploits the saxophone's capabilities to the maximum, in a way Glazunov would never have dreamed of. Flutter tones, slap-tonguing (a method that produces a percussive effect on a tone), and extensive use of the extreme upper register—devices that when left in other hands become mere gimmicks, or musical parlor tricks—are here used in perfect proportion, and with exceptional taste. Indeed, the tessiatura is quite startling, especially when played by someone with the capabilities of a Lawrence Gwozdz. Von Koch has a rich harmonic palette, and a deep, pure well of melodic ideas, always primary in his compositional schema.

The second movement is essentially a ternary song form with all three parts repeated in somewhat abridged manner with the recurrence of the first theme serving as a codetta. The saxophone line is extremely florid and vocal. One of the more interesting features of this movement is the rhythm—it tends to gather, almost imperceptibly, a forward, quickening motion over a long arch before putting on the brakes. The use of mixed-meter—twelve-eight, nine-eight, six-eight, five-eight—aids in the effect.

Once again, like Glazunov, von Koch could not resist incorporating materials from his earlier movements—indeed, basing the entire third movement on them. To be sure, all sorts of techniques, retrograde, inversions, slight rhythmic alterations, are used to accomplish this. But he pulls it off in this wonderful rondo in such a manner that we don't realize—at least for a while—that the joke is on us. In fact, some of the modalities and rhythmic turns remind us of another composer who wrote a famous saxophone concerto—Jacques Ibert. The mood is lighter, sprightly, and carefree, and not even the verbatim appearance of the opening theme of the first movement can dampen the spirit of this delightful piece, indeed, this sensationally delightful concerto.

—Steven Ritter

to Sigurd M. Rascher

Saxophone Concerto

I.

Erland von Koch
composed 1958

14

16

II.

III.

Allegro vivace (♩=ca 144)

14 Allegro vivace

stringendo al fine

ADVANCED ALTO SAX SOLOS – VOLUME 1

Performed by Paul Brodie, alto saxophone
Accompaniment: Antonin Kubalek, piano

Virtuoso Paul Brodie introduces you to the world of advanced alto sax solos with this wide-ranging collection. Contains performance suggestions and Mr. Brodie's incredible interpretations to help you achieve greatness! Includes a printed music score containing the solo part, annotated with performance suggestions; and access to professional recordings with complete versions (with soloist) followed by piano accompaniments to each piece, minus the soloist. Includes works by Vivaldi, Jacob, Whitney, and Benson.

00400602 Book/Online Audio...**$16.99**

ADVANCED ALTO SAX SOLOS – VOLUME 2

Performed by Vincent Abato, alto saxophone
Accompaniment: Harriet Wingreen, piano

Listen as extraordinary virtuoso Vincent Abato of the Metropolitan Opera Orchestra takes you further into the advanced repertoire with these spectacular sax selections. Listen to his masterful interpretations, examine his performance suggestions, then you step in and make magic with Harriet Wingreen, legendary piano accompanist for the New York Philharmonic. Includes: Schubert "The Bee," Rabaud "Solo de Concours," and Creston "Sonata, Op. 19" 2nd and 3rd movements. Includes a printed music score containing the solo part, annotated with performance suggestions; and tracks with complete versions (with soloist) followed by piano accompaniments to each piece, minus the soloist.

00400603 Book/Online Audio...**$16.99**

PLAY THE MUSIC OF
BURT BACHARACH
ALTO OR TENOR SAXOPHONE

Along with lyricist Hal David, Burt Bacharach penned some of the best pop songs and standards of all time. These superb collections let solo instrumentalists play along with: Alfie • Blue on Blue • Do You Know the Way to San Jose • I Say a Little Prayer • Magic Moments • This Guy's in Love with You • Walk on By • What the World Needs Now • The Windows of the World • and Wives and Lovers.

00400657 Book/Online Audio...**$22.99**

BOSSA, BONFÁ & BLACK ORPHEUS
FOR TENOR SAXOPHONE – A TRIBUTE
TO STAN GETZ
TENOR SAXOPHONE

featuring Glenn Zottola

Original transcriptions for you to perform! The bossa novas that swept the world in 1950 created a whole new set of songs to equal the great standards of the '20s, '30s and '40s by Gershwin, Porter, Arlen, Berlin, Kern and Rodgers. This collection for tenor sax is a tribute to the great Stan Getz and includes: Black Orpheus • Girl from Ipanema • Gentle Rain • One Note Samba • Once I Loved • Dindi • Baubles, Bangles and Beads • Meditation • Triste • I Concentrate on You • Samba de Orfeu.

00124387 Book/Online Audio...**$16.99**

CLASSIC STANDARDS FOR
ALTO SAXOPHONE
A TRIBUTE TO JOHNNY HODGES

featuring Bob Wilber

Ten classic standards are presented in this book as they were arranged for the Neal Hefti String Orchestra in 1954, including: Yesterdays • Laura • What's New? • Blue Moon • Can't Help Lovin' Dat Man • Embraceable You • Willow Weep for Me • Memories of You • Smoke Gets in Your Eyes • Stardust. Bob Wilber performs the songs on the provided CD on soprano saxophone, although they are translated for alto saxophone.

00131389 Book/Online Audio...**$16.99**

EASY JAZZ DUETS FOR 2 ALTO
SAXOPHONES AND RHYTHM SECTION

Performed by Hal McKusick, alto saxophone
Accompaniment: The Benny Goodman Rhythm Section:
George Duvivier, bass; Bobby Donaldson, drums

This great collection of jazz duets gives you the opportunity to accompany saxophonist Hal McKusick and the Benny Goodman Rhythm Section. Suitable for beginning players, all the selections are great fun. This album allows you to play either duet part. Includes printed musical score with access to online audio tracks: you hear both parts played in stereo, then each duet is repeated with the first part omitted and then the second part, so you can play along.

00400480 Book/Online Audio...**$16.99**

FROM DIXIE TO SWING
CLARINET OR SOPRANO SAX

Performed by Kenny Davern, clarinet
Accompaniment: Kenny Davern, clarinet & soprano sax; 'Doc' Cheatham, trumpet; Vic Dickenson, trombone; Dick Wellstood, piano; George Duvivier, bass; Gus Johnson Jr., drums

Such jazz legends as Dick Wellstood, Alphonse 'Doc' Cheatham and George Duvivier and more back you up in this amazing collection of New York-style Dixieland standards. After the break-up of the big-band era around 1950, many of the finest 'swing' or mainstream players found themselves without an outlet for their abilities and took to playing 'Dixieland' in New York clubs such as Eddie Condon's and the Metropole. And so was born a new style of Dixieland jazz minus the banjos, tubas, steamboats and magnolias! It is this version we celebrate on this album. We encourage you, the soloist, to invent counter-melodies rather than mere harmony parts. This is a music of loose weaving parts, not one of precision ensemble figures. And in short, it is one of the greatest improvisational experiences any jazz player could hope to have. Includes a printed music score and online audio access to stereo accompaniments to each piece.

00400613 Book/Online Audio...**$16.99**

GLAZUNOV – CONCERTO IN E-FLAT
MAJOR, OP. 109; VON KOCH –
CONCERTO IN E-FLAT MAJOR
ALTO SAXOPHONE

Performed by Lawrence Gwozdz, alto saxophone
Accompaniment: Plovdiv Philharmonic Orchestra
Conductor: Nayden Todorov

Alexander Glazunov, one of the great masters of late Russian Romanticism, was fascinated by the saxophone and by jazz. In 1934 he wrote this beautiful saxophone concerto which has become a classic, combining romanticism with modern idioms as well. Erland von Koch's 1958 saxophone concerto is filled with experimental modern tonalities and fantastic effects for the saxophone. Both are must-haves for the serious saxophonist. Includes a printed music score; informative liner notes; and online audio featuring the concerti performed twice: first with soloist, then again with orchestral accompaniment only, minus you, the soloist. The audio is accessed online using the unique code inside each book and can be streamed or downloaded.

00400487 Book/Online Audio...**$16.99**

To see a full listing of Music Minus One publications, visit
www.halleonard.com/MusicMinusOne

Prices, contents, and availability subject to change without notice.